Twen

Ti

to

Sach

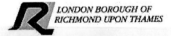

Search Press

Dedication
To mum.

First published in 2021

Search Press Limited
Wellwood, North Farm Road,
Tunbridge Wells, Kent TN2 3DR

Text copyright © Sachiyo Ishii, 2021

Photographs by Fiona Murray

Photographs and design copyright
© Search Press Ltd. 2021

ISBN: 978-1-78221-858-6
eBook: 978-1-78126-298-6

Publisher's Note

The Publishers and author can accept no
responsibility for any consequences arising from
the information, advice or instructions given in
this publication.

Readers are permitted to reproduce any
of the items in this book for their personal use,
or for the purposes of selling for charity, free of
charge and without the prior permission of the
Publishers. Any use of the items for commercial
purposes is not permitted without the prior
permission of the Publishers.

Suppliers

If you have difficulty in obtaining any of
the materials and equipment mentioned
in this book, then please visit the Search Press
website for details of suppliers:
www.searchpress.com

Contents

Introduction

My earliest memory of crochet is the crocheted baby booties my mother used to make. They were made in soft pastel colours and had bear faces crocheted on top. It was her part-time job which allowed her to stay home and look after my little brother and me. I loved these little booties and wished that I was small enough to wear them! It was amazing to watch strands of yarn take shape with a simple hook. It was magic.

It took me years to discover the joy of crochet myself. I always associated crochet with rather complicated diagrams, and the even more confusing US and UK terminology and abbreviations. I was puzzled and had given up even before I tried; but then I started seeing lots of amigurumi work on the internet. It was about time to have a go at this craft.

'Amigurumi' is the Japanese art of crocheting small stuffed creatures. 'Ami' means crocheted or knitted, and 'gurumi' means a stuffed toy. It is more common to crochet toys in Japan; for that reason, 'amigurumi' are usually crocheted toys.

So, is amigurumi difficult? Not at all! I don't know why I didn't learn to crochet much earlier. Crochet stitches are not too complicated, and once you know the basics it is simple and fun. You don't need to be an expert – start with a small ring of stitches, and with a series of increases and decreases the creature takes shape on its own. Most amigurumi are made with double crochet (US single crochet) stitches, made in a round, with each round 'spiralling' to the next to make the finished shape. For ease, I have joined each round with slip stitches so that no stitch markers are needed. Unlike many crochet patterns, there is also no need to read diagrams with amigurumi.

It is also easy to make your own amigurumi designs. With knitting, you often do not know the finish until you sew up and stuff, but with crochet, you can see the size and shape as you progress.

If you have never tried the craft before, have a go and explore. These little creatures are irresistible.

Happy crocheting!

Crochet know-how

Materials & tools

Yarn

Most of the toys in this book are crocheted with 4-ply (fingering) yarn, though some feature sections worked in DK (8-ply/light worsted) yarn. I prefer to use 4-ply (fingering) for small toy projects since crochet makes a quite dense fabric but, of course, you can use any weight of yarn you like. You only need small amounts to create each toy – perfect for using up yarn already in your stash.

For the samples in the book I have used synthetic yarns made from a blend of nylon and acrylic, with a yardage of 50g per 180–220m (197–219yd). However, feel free to experiment with any yarn you like.

Stuffing

I have used polyester toy stuffing, which is readily available from most bricks-and-mortar craft shops and online craft stores. Stuff the toys relatively lightly to keep them nice and soft.

Beads

4–6mm (⅙–¼in) mushroom beads are used as eyes for a number of projects. I prefer to use beads with threading holes and attach them after the head is stuffed. If you are making the toy for a child, embroider French knots for the eyes using black DK (8-ply/light worsted) yarn. Alternatively, use safety eyes in place of the beads and attach them before stuffing the head.

Wire

Some of the projects, such as the Robot and Whales, have features made with craft wire. For the size of the toys I recommend a finer gauge, such as 24 gauge (0.51mm). If these makes are for very young children, omit the wire.

Crochet hook

All the toys in this book were made using a 3mm (UK 11, US C2/D3) crochet hook. Your crochet tension needs to be fairly tight so that the stuffing is not visible through the stitches once the toy is made up. I found this hook size the most suitable for amigurumi projects, especially when using 4-ply (fingering) yarn. It goes through stitches smoothly and does not split the yarn.

I like using a hook with a handle. They are ergonomically designed and offer a better grip. If you suffer from pain associated with yarn crafting, it may be a good idea to try out different crochet hooks.

Chenille needle

Essential for sewing up and assembling your amigurumi toys – see the technique, below.

Scissors

A pair of sharp scissors is essential for trimming yarn ends when sewing up your projects.

Other useful tools

All-purpose sewing needle

I use this to attach the eyes or beads.

Row/round counter

This can be useful to keep count of your rows and rounds, as it's sometimes difficult to see them.

Wooden chopstick

A simple but incredibly effective tool, a chopstick is by far the best instrument for pushing stuffing into your toys. If your crochet hook has a large grip handle, you can use it as well.

Pliers

For twisting wire more easily.

Fabric glue

For attaching non-crocheted features like felt.

Techniques

Sewing your work together

I recommend that you use a chenille needle for sewing up as it has a sharper point, making it easier to work through your tightly knitted toys than a blunt-ended needle. You can also use the same needle for embroidering features on the toys, too. Your toys will be sewn up using the same yarn that you crocheted them with, so it is a good idea to make a habit of leaving fairly long yarn ends when you cast on and fasten off. Join the seams by weaving through the fastened-off edge to close the work tightly. Weave in any remaining loose ends, and cut excess yarn flush against the crochet – the tail of yarn will shrink inside.

Stitches used

An adjustable/magic ring

Wrap yarn around your forefinger to make a loop. Insert the hook into the circle, wrap the working yarn over your hook from back to front and draw the yarn through. Continue holding the circle of yarn as you make a turning chain, yarn over from back to front, draw the hook through the loop on the hook to complete a chain stitch. Insert the hook into the ring, yarn over and draw up a loop, yarn over and draw the yarn through both loops on your hook to finish the first double crochet stitch. When you make the double crochet stitches required in the first round, join the ring by making a slip stitch to the first chain and draw the yarn tail tight to close the ring.

Double crochet (US single crochet)

Most patterns are worked in double crochet in this book. This is the easiest stitch to crochet, and once you have learnt it there are many possible ways to use it. Insert the hook through the adjustable ring or foundation chain, wrap the yarn over your crochet hook then draw the hook and working yarn through the ring or chain loops. Wrap the yarn around the hook again and draw the yarn through both loops.

Half treble crochet (US half double crochet)

Wind the yarn around the hook. Insert the hook under the top two loops of the next stitch in the previous round or row, then wrap the yarn around the hook again. Pull the yarn through the stitch only (three loops on the hook), wind the yarn around the hook, then pull the yarn through all three loops.

Treble crochet (US double crochet)

Insert the hook under the top two loops of the stitch on the previous round or row. Wrap the yarn around the hook and pull the yarn through the stitch only (three loops on the

hook). Wrap the yarn around the hook again and draw the yarn through just the first two loops on the hook (two loops on the hook). Wrap the yarn around the hook once more then draw the yarn through the remaining loops on the hook.

Double treble crochet (US treble crochet)

Wrap the yarn around the hook twice and insert the hook under the top two loops of the stitch on the previous round or row. Wrap the yarn around the hook once then pull the yarn through the first two of the four loops on the hook (three loops on the hook). Wrap the yarn around the hook, then draw it through the first two loops on the hook (two loops on the hook), yarn over the hook once more then draw through the last two loops on the hook.

UK/US crochet stitch conversions

Only UK crochet terms are used in the patterns throughout this book. For US conversions, please refer to the table below. The stitches listed below are the most frequently used; any special stitches or techniques in a pattern are explained on the relevant page.

UK		US	
dc	double crochet	**sc**	single crochet
htr	half treble crochet	**hdc**	half double crochet
tr	treble crochet	**dc**	double crochet
dtr	double treble crochet	**tr**	treble crochet
tbl	through back loop	**tbl**	through back loop
tension		**gauge**	
miss		**skip**	
adjustable ring		**magic ring**	

Robot

Materials (for one robot)

65m (72yd) of 4-ply (fingering) weight yarn in sky-blue (A) or pink (B)

Small amounts of 4-ply (fingering) weight yarn in white (C), yellow (D), bright green (E)

30cm (12in) length of fine craft wire

Two 6mm (¼in) black beads, for the eyes

Black cotton thread, for sewing the beads

Optional: small amount of black yarn, for embroidering the eyes

Tools

3mm (UK 11, US C2/D3) crochet hook

Chenille needle

All-purpose sewing needle, if using beads

Pliers

Scissors

Size

9cm (3½in)

Instructions (to make one robot)

Body

Round 1: with yarn A or B and working into an adjustable ring, 6 dc, join with a sl st (6 sts).

Round 2: 1 ch, (2 dc in next st) to end, join with a sl st (12 sts).

Round 3: 1 ch, (1 dc, 2 dc in next st) to end, join with a sl st (18 sts).

Round 4: 1 ch, (2 dc, 2 dc in next st) to end, join with a sl st (24 sts).

Round 5: 1 ch, (3 dc, 2 dc in next st) to end, join with a sl st (30 sts).

Round 6 (tbl): 1 ch, 1 dc in each st around, join with a sl st.

Rounds 7–15: 1 ch, 1 dc in each st around, join with a sl st.

Round 16 (tbl): 1 ch, 1 dc in each st around, join with a sl st.

Round 17: 1 ch, (3 dc, dc2tog) to end, join with a sl st (24 sts).

Round 18: 1 ch, (2 dc, dc2tog) to end, join with a sl st (18 sts).

Round 19: 1 ch, (1 dc, dc2tog) to end, join with a sl st (12 sts). Stuff.

Round 20: 1 ch, (dc2tog) six times, join with a sl st (6 sts). Fasten off.

Head

With yarn A or B, work as body to round 5 (30 sts).

Rounds 6–11: 1 ch, 1 dc in each st around, join with a sl st.

Round 12 (tbl): 1 ch, 1 dc in each st around, join with a sl st.

Round 13: 1 ch, 1 dc in each st around, join with a sl st.

Rounds 14–17: work as rounds 17–20 of body. Fasten off.

Foot (make two)

Work as body to round 3 (18 sts).

Rounds 4–7: 1 ch, 1 dc in each st around, join with a sl st.

Round 8 (tbl): 1 ch, 1 dc in each st around, join with a sl st.

Rounds 9 and 10: work as rounds 19 and 20 of body. Stuff.

Fasten off.

Arm (make two)

Work as body to round 2 (12 sts).

Round 3 (tbl): 1 ch, 1 dc in each st around, join with a sl st.

Rounds 4–8: 1 ch, 1 dc in each st around, join with a sl st.

Round 9 (tbl): 1 ch, 1 dc in each st around, join with a sl st. Stuff.

Round 10: 1 ch, dc2tog six times, join with a sl st (6 sts).

Fasten off.

Button (make four)

Round 1: with yarn A, B, C, D or E and working into an adjustable ring, 6 dc, join with a sl st (6 sts).

Fasten off.

Making up

Sew eyes onto the head – use the beads and black cotton thread, or make the eyes by embroidering French knots with the black yarn.

Sew the buttons to body.

From the craft wire cut a 5cm (2in) length and wrap it with yarn C. Bend one end into a circle shape and insert the other straight end into the bottom of the arm. Secure the wire to the arm with several stitches. Repeat for the other arm.

For the antenna, cut the wire to a 7cm (3in) length and wrap it with yarn C, leaving a long tail. Bend one end into a circle or heart shape then insert the other end into the head together with the yarn tail, using the needle to help you. Take the yarn out from the bottom of the head and use it make a few stitches at the base of the antenna to secure it to the head.

Attach all body parts to the body.

Weave in any loose ends to finish.

Stripy Kitten

Materials

Small amounts of 4-ply (fingering) weight yarn in orange (A), white (B), light brown (C), dark brown (D)

Two 5mm (³⁄₁₆in) black beads, for the eyes

Black cotton thread, for sewing the beads

Toy stuffing

Optional: small amount of black yarn, for embroidering the eyes

Tools

3mm (UK 11, US C2/D3) crochet hook

Chenille needle

All-purpose sewing needle, for sewing on the beads

Scissors

Size

7.5cm (3in)

Instructions

Head

Round 1: with yarn B and working into an adjustable ring, 7 dc, join with a sl st (7 sts).

Round 2: 1 ch, 2 dc in each st around, join with a sl st (14 sts).

Round 3: 1 ch, 1 dc in each st around, join with a sl st.

Change to yarn A. Break yarn B.

Round 4: 1 ch, 5 dc, (2 dc in next st) four times, 5 dc, join with a sl st (18 sts).

Round 5: 1 ch, (2 dc, 2 dc in next st) to end, join with a sl st (24 sts).

Round 6: 1 ch, 9 dc, join yarn C, 1 dc in yarn C, 1 dc in yarn A, 1 dc in yarn C, 1 dc in yarn A, 1 dc in yarn C, 10 dc in yarn A, join with a sl st.

Rounds 7 and 8: with colours as set, 1 ch, 1 dc in each st around, join with a sl st.

Round 9: 1 ch, with colours correct, (3 dc, 2 dc in next st) to end, join with a sl st (30 sts).

Round 10: with colours as set, 1 ch, 1 dc in each st around, join with a sl st.

Break yarn C. Work with yarn A only.

Round 11: 1 ch, (3 dc, dc2tog) to end, join with a sl st (24 sts).

Round 12: 1 ch, (2 dc, dc2tog) to end, join with a sl st (18 sts).

Round 13: 1 ch, (1 dc, dc2tog) to end, join with a sl st (12 sts). Stuff.

Round 14: 1 ch, (dc2tog) six times, join with a sl st (6 sts). Fasten off.

Ear (make two)

Round 1: with yarn A and working into an adjustable ring, 5 dc, join with a sl st (5 sts).

Round 2: 1 ch, 1 dc in each st around, join with a sl st.

Round 3: 1 ch, 1 dc, (2 dc in next st, 1 dc) twice, join with a sl st (7 sts).

Round 4: 1 ch, 1 dc in each st around, join with a sl st.

Fasten off.

Body

Round 1: with yarn C and working into an adjustable ring, 6 dc, join with a sl st (6 sts).

Round 2: 1 ch, 2 dc in each st around, join with a sl st (12 sts).

Round 3: 1 ch, (1 dc, 2 dc in next st) to end, join with a sl st (18 sts).

Round 4: 1 ch, (2 dc, 2 dc in next st) to end, join with a sl st (24 sts).

Round 5: 1 ch, 1 dc in each st around, join with a sl st.

Round 6: join yarn A, 1 ch, 1 dc in each st around, join with a sl st.

Round 7: with yarn C, 1 ch, 1 dc in each st around, join with a sl st.

Round 8: with yarn A, 1 ch, (2 dc, dc2tog) to end, join with a sl st (18 sts).

Round 9: with yarn C, 1 dc in each st around, join with a sl st.

Round 10: with yarn A, 1 ch, 1 dc in each st around, join with a sl st.

Round 11: with yarn C, 1 ch, 1 dc in each st around, join with a sl st.

Round 12: with yarn A, 1 ch, (1 dc, dc2tog) to end, join with a sl st (12 sts).

Fasten off.

Arm (make two)

Round 1: with yarn A and working into an adjustable ring, 6 dc, join with a sl st (6 sts).

Round 2: 1 ch, 1 dc in each st around, join with a sl st.

Round 3: join yarn C, 1 ch, 1 dc in each st around, join with a sl st.

Rounds 4–6: alternating colours in every round, 1 ch, 1 dc in each st around, join with a sl st.

Fasten off.

Leg (make two)

Round 1: with yarn A and working into an adjustable ring, 5 dc, join with a sl st (5 sts).

Round 2: 1 ch, 2 dc in each st around, join with a sl st (10 sts).

Round 3: 1 ch, 3 dc, 4 htr, 3 dc, join with a sl st.

Round 4: 1 ch, 3 dc, (htr2tog) twice, 3 dc, join with a sl st (8 sts).

Rounds 5–7: 1 ch, 1 dc in each st around, join with a sl st.

Fasten off.

Tail

Round 1: with yarn B and working into an adjustable ring, 6 dc, join with a sl st (6 sts).

Rounds 2 and 3: 1 ch, 1 dc in each st around, join with a sl st. Change to yarn A.

Rounds 4–8: 1 ch, 1 dc in each st around, join with a sl st. Fasten off.

Making up

Sew the ears to the head.

Sew eyes onto the head – use the beads and black cotton thread, or make the eyes by embroidering French knots with the black yarn. To finish the head, embroider the nose onto the face with yarn D.

Stuff the body, arms and legs. Attach the arms, legs, tail and head to the body.

Weave in any loose ends to finish.

Bear

Materials (for one bear)

Small amounts of 4-ply (fingering) weight yarn in light brown or beige (A), white (B), aqua blue (C), coral pink (D), dark brown (E)

Two 4mm (⅛in) black beads, for the eyes

Black cotton thread, for sewing the beads

Two circles of medium-pink felt, 5mm (³⁄₁₆in) in diameter

Toy stuffing

Optional: small amount of black yarn, for embroidering the eyes

Tools

3mm (UK 11, US C2/D3) crochet hook

Chenille needle

All-purpose sewing needle, for sewing on the beads

Scissors

Fabric glue

Size

7.5cm (3in)

Instructions (to make one bear)

Body

Round 1: with yarn A and working into an adjustable ring, 6 dc, join with a sl st (6 sts).

Round 2: 1 ch, 2 dc in each st around, join with a sl st (12 sts).

Round 3: 1 ch, (1 dc, 2 dc in next st) to end, join with a sl st (18 sts).

Round 4: 1 ch, (2 dc, 2 dc in next st) to end, join with a sl st (24 sts).

Rounds 5–7: 1 ch, 1 dc in each st around, join with a sl st.

Round 8: 1 ch, (2 dc, dc2tog) to end, join with a sl st (18 sts).

Rounds 9 and 10: 1 ch, 1 dc in each st around, join with a sl st.

Round 11: 1 ch, (1 dc, dc2tog) to end, join with a sl st (12 sts).

Fasten off.

Head

Work as for body to round 4 (24 sts).

Round 5: 1 ch, (3 dc, 2 dc in next st) to end, join with a sl st (30 sts).

Rounds 6–9: 1 ch, 1 dc in each st around, join with a sl st.

Round 10: 1 ch, (3 dc, dc2tog) to end, join with a sl st (24 sts).

Round 11: 1 ch, (2 dc, dc2tog) to end, join with a sl st (18 sts).

Round 12: 1 ch, (1 dc, dc2tog) to end, join with a sl st (12 sts). Stuff.

Round 13: 1 ch, (dc2tog) six times, join with a sl st (6 sts).

Fasten off.

Muzzle

Round 1: with yarn A or B and working into an adjustable ring, 6 dc, join with a sl st (6 sts).

Round 2: 1 ch, 2 dc in each st around, join with a sl st (12 sts).

Rounds 3 and 4: 1 ch, 1 dc in each st. Fasten off.

Ear (make two)

Row 1: with yarn B and working into an adjustable ring, 5 dc. Do not join with a sl st, turn. Change to yarn A.

Row 2: 1 ch, 2 dc in each st around (10 sts).

Fasten off.

Leg (make two)

Round 1: with yarn A and working into an adjustable ring, 5 dc, join with a sl st (5 sts).

Round 2: 1 ch, 2 dc in each st around, join with a sl st (10 sts).

Round 3: 1 ch, 1 dc in each st to end, join with a sl st.

Round 4: 1 ch, 3 dc, (dc2tog) twice, 3 dc, join with a sl st (8 sts).

Rounds 5–7: 1 ch, 1 dc in each st, join with sl st.

Fasten off.

Arm (make two)

Round 1: with yarn A and working into an adjustable ring, 8 dc, join with sl st (8 sts).

Rounds 2–5: 1 ch, 1 dc in each st to end, join with a sl st.

Fasten off.

Trousers

With yarn C or D, work as for body to round 4 (24 sts).

Rounds 5–7: 1 ch, 1 dc in each st to end, join with a sl st.

Round 8: 1 ch, (2 dc, 1 dc2tog) to end, join with a sl st (18 sts).

Fasten off.

Trouser strap (make two)

With yarn C or D (so it matches the trousers), make 14 ch.

Fasten off.

Making up

Stuff the muzzle then attach it to the head. Attach the ears.

Sew eyes onto the head – use the beads and black cotton thread, or make the eyes by embroidering French knots with the black yarn. Embroider a nose and mouth onto the head with yarn E. Glue the felt circles onto the head to make cheeks.

Stuff the body. Slip the body into the trousers. Stuff the arms and legs then attach them to the body. Sew on the trouser straps, crossing them over at the back. Attach the head to the body.

Weave in any loose ends to finish.

Dinosaur

Materials

50m (55yd) of DK (8-ply/light worsted) weight yarn in green (A)

Small amount of DK (8-ply/light worsted) weight yarn in soft yellow (B)

Two 6mm (¼in) black beads, for the eyes

Black cotton thread, for sewing the beads

Two circles of light-pink felt, 5mm (³⁄₁₆in) in diameter

Toy stuffing

Optional: small amount of black yarn, for embroidering the eyes

Tools

3mm (UK 11, US C2/D3) crochet hook

Chenille needle

All-purpose sewing needle, for sewing on the beads

Scissors

Fabric glue

Size

10cm (4in)

Instructions

Body

Round 1: with yarn A and working into an adjustable ring, 6 dc, join with a sl st (6 sts).

Round 2: 1 ch, 2 dc in each st around, join with a sl st (12 sts).

Round 3: 1 ch, (1 dc, 2 dc in next st) to end, join with a sl st (18 sts).

Round 4: 1 ch, (2 dc, 2 dc in next st) to end, join with a sl st (24 sts).

Round 5: 1 ch, (3 dc, 2 dc in next st) to end, join with a sl st (30 sts).

Round 6: 1 ch, (4 dc, 2 dc in next st) to end, join with a sl st (36 sts).

Rounds 7–10: 1 ch, 1 dc in each st around, join with a sl st.

Rounds 11–14: 1 ch, dc2tog, 1 dc in each st around to last 2 sts, dc2tog, join with a sl st (28 sts).

Rounds 15 and 16: 1 ch, 1 dc in each st around, join with a sl st.

Round 17: 1 ch, dc2tog, 1 dc in each st around to last 2 sts, dc2tog, join with a sl st (26 sts).

Round 18: 1 ch, 1 dc in each st around, join with a sl st.

Round 19: 1 ch, 2 dc, (dc2tog, 2 dc) to end, join with a sl st (20 sts).

Round 20: 1 ch, 1 dc in each st around, join with a sl st.

Round 21: 1 ch, (2 dc, dc2tog) to end, join with a sl st (15 sts).

Fasten off.

Head

Work as for body to round 5 (30 sts).

Rounds 6–8: 1 ch, 1 dc in each st around, join with a sl st.

Round 9: 1 ch, (3 dc, dc2tog) to end, join with a sl st (24 sts).

Round 10: 1 ch, (2 dc, dc2tog) to end, join with a sl st (18 sts).

Round 11: 1 ch, 1 dc in each st around, join with a sl st.

Round 12: 1 ch, (1 dc, dc2tog) to end, join with a sl st (12 sts). Stuff.

Round 13: 1 ch, (dc2tog) six times, join with a sl st (6 sts).

Fasten off.

Tail

Round 1: with yarn A and working into an adjustable ring, 6 dc, join with a sl st (6 sts).

Rounds 2–4: 1 ch, 1 dc in each st around, join with a sl st.

Round 5: 1 ch, (2 dc, 2 dc in next st) to end, join with a sl st (8 sts).

Round 6: 1 ch, 1 dc in each st around, join with a sl st.

Round 7: 1 ch, (3 dc, 2 dc in next st) to end, join with a sl st (10 sts).

Round 8: 1 ch, (1 dc, 2 dc in next st) to end, join with a sl st (15 sts).

Rounds 9 and 10: 1 ch, 1 dc in each st around, join with a sl st.

Fasten off.

Leg (make two)

Work as for body to round 3 (18 sts).

Rounds 4 and 5: 1 ch, 1 dc in each st around, join with a sl st.

Fasten off.

Arm (make two)

Round 1: with yarn A and working into an adjustable ring, 7 dc, join with a sl st (7 sts).

Rounds 2–6: 1 ch, 1 dc in each st around, join with a sl st.

Fasten off.

Spikes

With yarn B, make 32 ch.

Starting in third ch from hook, *1 htr, 1 tr, 1 dtr, 1 htr, sl st; repeat from * four more times, **1 dc, 1 htr; repeat from ** once more.

Fasten off.

Making up

Stuff the body.

Sew eyes onto the head – use the beads and black cotton thread, or make the eyes by embroidering French knots with black yarn. Stuff the arms and legs then attach them to the body.

Stuff the tail and attach it to the body. Sew the spikes to the body. With yarn B, embroider lines onto the tummy. Glue the circles of pink felt onto the head to make cheeks.

Weave in any loose ends to finish.

Helicopter

Materials

Small amounts of DK (8-ply/light
worsted) weight yarn in white (A),
light blue (B), blue (C), yellow
green (D), dark pink (E)

Toy stuffing

Tools

3mm (UK 11, US C2/D3)
crochet hook

Chenille needle

Scissors

Size

11cm (4½in) long

Instructions

Top inner compartment (window)

Round 1: with yarn A and working
into an adjustable ring, 6 dc, join with
a sl st (6 sts).

Round 2: 1 ch, 2 dc in next st to end,
join with a sl st (12 sts).

Round 3: 1 ch, (1 dc, 2 dc in next st)
to end, join with a sl st (18 sts).

Round 4: 1 ch, (2 dc, 2 dc in next st)
to end, join with a sl st (24 sts).

Round 5: 1 ch, (3 dc, 2 dc in next st)
to end, join with a sl st (30 sts).

Round 6: 1 ch, (4 dc, 2 dc in next st)
to end, join with a sl st (36 sts).

Rounds 7–12: 1 ch, 1 dc in each st
around, join with a sl st.

Round 13 (tbl): 1 ch, 1 dc in each st
around, join with a sl st.

Round 14: 1 ch, (4 dc, dc2tog) to
end, join with a sl st (30 sts).

Round 15: 1 ch, (3 dc, dc2tog) to
end, join with a sl st (24 sts).

Round 16: 1 ch, (2 dc, dc2tog) to
end, join with a sl st (18 sts).

Round 17: 1 ch, (1 dc, dc2tog) to
end, join with a sl st (12 sts). Stuff.

Round 18: 1 ch, (dc2tog) six times,
join with a sl st (6 sts).

Fasten off.

Top outer compartment

With yarn B, work as inner piece to
round 6 (36 sts).

Round 7: 1 ch, (5 dc, 2 dc in next st)
to end, join with a sl st (42 sts).

Round 8 (tbl): 1 ch, 1 dc in each st
around, join with a sl st.

Round 9: 1 ch, 1 dc in each st
around, join with a sl st.

Fasten off.

Join in yarn B with a sl st yarn in tenth
st from last st on the right-hand side.

Row 1: 1 ch, 18 dc, turn (18 sts).

Rows 2–6: 1 ch, 1 dc in each st to
end, turn.

Row 7: 1 ch, (4 dc, dc2tog) to end,
turn (15 sts).

Row 8: 1 ch, (3 dc, dc2tog) to end,
turn (12 sts).

Row 9: 1 ch, (2 dc, dc2tog) to end,
turn (9 sts).

Row 10: 1 ch, (1 dc, dc2tog) to end,
turn (6 sts). Fasten off.

Propeller (make two)

Round 1: with yarn E and working
into an adjustable ring, 6 dc, join with
a sl st (6 sts).

Round 2: 1 ch, 2 dc in next st to end,
join with a sl st (12 sts).

Rounds 3 and 4: 1 ch, 1 dc in each
st around, join with a sl st.

Round 5: 1 ch, (4 dc, dc2tog) twice,
join with a sl st (10 sts).

Round 6: 1 ch, (3 dc, dc2tog) twice,
join with a sl st (8 sts).

Round 7: 1 ch, (2 dc, dc2tog) twice,
join with a sl st (6 sts).

Fasten off.

Top bobble

With yarn C, work as for propeller to
round 2 (12 sts).

Round 3: 1 ch, 1 dc in each st, join
with a sl st.

Round 4: 1 ch, (dc2tog) six times,
join with a sl st (6 sts).

Fasten off.

Tail

Round 1: with yarn D and working
into an adjustable ring, 6 dc, join with a
sl st (6 sts).

Round 2: 1 ch, (2 dc, 2 dc in next st)
twice, join with a sl st (8 sts).

Round 3: 1 ch, (3 dc, 2 dc in next st)
twice, join with a sl st (10 sts).

Rounds 4–7: 1 ch, 1 dc in each st
around, join with a sl st.

Round 8: 1 ch, (4 dc, 2 dc in next st)
twice, join with a sl st (12 sts).

Fasten off.

Tail bobble

With yarn C, work as for propeller to
round 2 (12 sts).

Rounds 3 and 4: 1 ch, 1 dc in each st
around, join with a sl st. Stuff.

Round 5: 1 ch, (dc2tog) six times, join
with a sl st (6 sts). Fasten off.

Base bobble

Work as top bobble, using yarn B.

Helicopter foot (make two)

With yarn C, make 4 ch.

Row 1: starting in second ch from
hook, 1 dc in each ch, turn (3 sts).

Rows 2–23: 1 ch, 1 dc in each st, turn.

Fasten off.

Encase the top inner compartment inside the top outer compartment, stuff then secure the two together all around using yarn B.

Stuff the tail then sew it to the back of the top outer compartment. Sew the tail bobble to the end of the tail.

Sew the feet to the base bobble, then attach the base bobble to the base of the outer compartment. Sew the propellers on top of the outer compartment. Sew the top bobble centrally on top of the propellers.

Weave in any loose ends to finish.

Robin

Materials

Small amounts of DK (8-ply/light worsted) weight yarn in orange (A), soft brown (B), dark brown (C)

Two 5mm (³⁄₁₆in) black beads, for the eyes

Black cotton thread, for sewing the beads

Toy stuffing

Optional: small amount of black yarn, for embroidering the eyes

Tools

3mm (UK 11, US C2/D3) crochet hook

Chenille needle

All-purpose sewing needle, for sewing on the beads

Scissors

Size

4.5cm (1¾in)

Instructions

Body

Round 1: with yarn A and working into an adjustable ring, 6 dc, join with sl st (6 sts).

Round 2: 1 ch, 2 dc in each st around, join with sl st (12 sts).

Round 3: 1 ch, (1 dc, 2 dc in next st) to end, join with sl st (18 sts).

Round 4: 1 ch, (2 dc, 2 dc in next st) to end, join with sl st (24 sts).

Join yarn B.

Round 5: 1 ch, 9 dc in yarn B, (2 htr in next st) six times in yarn A, 9 dc in yarn B, join with sl st (30 sts).

Break yarn A and B. Join yarn C.

Round 6: 1 ch, 12 dc, 6 htr, 12 dc, join with sl st.

Rounds 7–9: 1 ch, 1 dc in each st around, join with sl st.

Round 10: 1 ch, 9 dc, (htr2tog) six times, 9 dc, join with sl st (24 sts).

Round 11: 1 ch, 8 dc, (htr2tog) four times, 8 dc, join with sl st (20 sts).

Round 12: 1 ch, 6 dc, (dc2tog) four times, 6 dc, join with sl st (16 sts).

Round 13: 1 ch, 4 dc, (dc2tog) four times, 4 dc, join with sl st (12 sts). Stuff.

Round 14: 1 ch, 2 dc, (dc2tog) four times, 2 dc, join with sl st (8 sts).

Round 15: 1 ch, 1 dc in each st around, join with sl st.

Round 16: 1 ch, (dc2tog) four times, join with sl st (4 sts).

Fasten off.

Wing (make two)

Round 1: with yarn C and working into an adjustable ring, 6 dc, join with sl st (6 sts).

Round 2: 1 ch, 2 dc in each st around, join with sl st (12 sts).

Round 3: 1 ch, 1 dc in each st around, join with sl st.

Round 4: 1 ch, (4 dc, dc2tog) twice, join with sl st (10 sts).

Round 5: 1 ch, (3 dc, dc2tog) twice, join with sl st (8 sts).

Round 6: 1 ch, (dc2tog) four times, join with sl st (4 sts). Fasten off.

Beak

Round 1: with yarn C and working into an adjustable ring, 4 dc.

Fasten off.

Making up

Weave through the finishing ends of the wings. Attach the wings to the body.

Attach the beak to the body.

Sew eyes onto the head – use the beads and black cotton thread, or make the eyes by embroidering French knots with the black yarn.

Weave in any loose ends to finish.

Car

Materials

18m (19¾yd) of DK (8-ply/light worsted) yarn in pink (A)

Small amounts of DK (8-ply/light worsted) weight yarn in sky blue (B), white (C), dark brown (D)

Small amounts of 4-ply (fingering) weight yarn in yellow (E), orange (F)

Toy stuffing

Tools

3mm (UK 11, US C2/D3) crochet hook

Chenille needle

Scissors

Size

6cm (2½in) tall

Instructions

Car body

Starting with the undercarriage and using yarn A, make 10 ch.

Round 1: starting in second ch from hook, 8 dc, 3 dc in last ch, working on the other side of ch, 7 dc, 2 dc in last ch, join with sl st (20 sts).

Round 2: 1 ch, 2 dc in first st, 7 dc, (2 dc in next st) three times, 7 dc, (2 dc in next st) twice, join with sl st (26 sts).

Round 3: 1 ch, 2 dc in first st, 8 dc, (2 dc in next st, 1 dc) three times, 7 dc, (2 dc in next st, 1 dc) twice, join with sl st (32 sts).

Round 4: 1 ch, 2 dc in first st, 9 dc, (2 dc in next st, 2 dc) three times, 7 dc, (2 dc in next st, 2 dc) twice, join with sl st (38 sts).

Round 5: 1 ch, 2 dc in first st, 10 dc, (2 dc in next st, 3 dc) three times, 7 dc, (2 dc in next st, 3 dc) twice, join with sl st (44 sts).

Continue, to make the main body of the car.

Round 6 (tbl): 1 ch, 1 dc in each st around, join with sl st.

Rounds 7–11: 1 ch, 1 dc in each st around, join with sl st.

Round 12: 1 ch, (9 dc, dc2tog) to end, join with sl st (40 sts).

Round 13: 1 ch, (3 dc, dc2tog) to end, join with sl st (32 sts).

Round 14: 1 ch, (2 dc, dc2tog) to end, join with sl st (24 sts).

Round 15: 1 ch, (2 dc, dc2tog) to end, join with sl st (18 sts).

Fasten off.

Window

Round 1: with yarn B and working into an adjustable ring, 6 dc, join with sl st (6 sts).

Round 2: 1 ch, 2 dc in each st around, join with sl st (12 sts).

Round 3: 1 ch, (1 dc, 2 dc in next st) to end, join (18 sts).

Round 4: 1 ch, (2 dc, 2 dc in next st) to end, join with sl st (24 sts).

Round 5: 1 ch, (3 dc, 2 dc in next st) to end, join with sl st (30 sts).

Rounds 6–10: 1 ch, 1 dc in each st around, join with sl st.

Round 11 (tbl): 1 ch, 1 dc in each st around, join with sl st.

Round 12: 1 ch, 1 dc in each st around, join with sl st.

Round 13: 1 ch, (3 dc, dc2tog) to end, join with sl st (24 sts).

Round 14: 1 ch, (2 dc, dc2tog) to end, join with sl st (18 sts).

Round 15: 1 ch, (1 dc, dc2tog) to end, join with sl st (12 sts). Stuff.

Round 16: 1 ch, (dc2tog) six times, join with sl st (6 sts).

Fasten off.

Roof

With yarn A, work as window to round 4 (24 sts).

Round 5: 1 ch, 1 dc in each st around, join with sl st.

Fasten off.

*Join yarn in seventh st from last st.

Row 1: 1 ch, 2 dc, turn (2 sts).

Row 2: 1 ch, 2 dc, turn.

Row 3: 1 ch, miss first st, 1 dc in second st (1 st). Make 2 ch.

Fasten off.

Repeat from * to end for the other side.

Wheel (make four)

With yarn C, work as for window to round 2 (12 sts).

Change to yarn D.

Round 3: 1 ch, (1 dc, 2 dc in next st) to end, join with sl st (18 sts).

Round 4: 1 ch, 1 dc in each st around, join with sl st.

Round 5: 1 ch, (1 dc, dc2tog) to end, join with sl st (12 sts).

Round 6: 1 ch, (dc2tog) six times, join with sl st (6 sts).

Fasten off.

Front light (make two)

With yarn E, work as for window to round 2 (12 sts).

Round 3: 1 ch, (dc2tog) six times, join with sl st (6 sts).

Fasten off.

Back light (make two)

With yarn E and working into an adjustable ring, 6 dc, join with sl st (6 sts). Fasten off.

Making up

Stuff the car body. Cover the window piece with the roof piece then secure the roof with a few stitches. Attach the window piece to the top of the car body. Attach the wheels and lights.

Weave in any loose ends to finish.

Penguin

Materials:

Small amounts of 4-ply (fingering) weight yarn in blue (A), white (B), orange (C)

Two 5mm (³⁄₁₆in) black beads, for the eyes

Black cotton thread, for sewing the beads

Toy stuffing

Optional: small amount of black yarn, for embroidering the eyes

Tools

3mm (UK 11, US C2/D3) crochet hook

Chenille needle

All-purpose sewing needle, for sewing on the beads

Scissors

Size

4.5cm (1¾in)

Instructions

Body

Round 1: with yarn B and working into an adjustable ring, 6 dc, join with sl st (6 sts).

Round 2: 1 ch, 2 dc in each st around, join with sl st (12 sts).

Round 3: 1 ch, (1 dc, 2 dc in next st) to end, join (18 sts).

Round 4: 1 ch, (2 dc, 2 dc in next st) to end, join with sl st (24 sts).

Change to yarn A.

Round 5: 1 ch, 9 dc, (2 htr in next st) six times, 9 dc, join with sl st (30 sts).

Round 6: 1 ch, 12 dc, 6 htr, 12 dc, join with sl st.

Rounds 7–9: 1 ch, 1 dc in each st around, join with sl st.

Round 10: 1 ch, 9 dc, (htr2tog) six times, 9 dc, join with sl st (24 sts).

Round 11: 1 ch, (2 dc, dc2tog) to end, join with sl st (18 sts).

Round 12: 1 ch, *1 dc, (dc2tog) twice, repeat from * to end, join with sl st (12 sts). Stuff.

Round 13: 1 ch, (dc2tog) six times, join with sl st (6 sts).

Fasten off.

Wing (make two)

Round 1: with yarn A and working into an adjustable ring, 6 dc, join with sl st (6 sts).

Round 2: 1 ch, 2 dc in each st around, join with sl st (12 sts).

Rounds 3–5: 1 ch, 1 dc in each st around, join with sl st.

Fasten off.

Beak

With yarn C and working into an adjustable ring, 5 dc.

Fasten off.

Making up

Weave through the finishing ends of the wings. Attach the wings to the body.

Attach the beak to the body.

Sew eyes onto the head – use the beads and black cotton thread, or make the eyes by embroidering French knots with the black yarn.

Weave in any loose ends to finish.

Chameleon

Materials

Small amounts of 4-ply (fingering) weight yarn in
    green (A), aqua blue (B), lilac (C), yellow green
    (D), dark brown (E), red (F), black (G)

Two 4mm (⅛in) black beads, for the eyes

Black cotton thread, for sewing the beads

Toy stuffing

Tools

3mm (UK 11, US C2/D3) crochet hook

Chenille needle

All-purpose sewing needle, for sewing on
    the beads

Scissors

Size

Chameleon – 10cm (4in) long

Ladybird – 1.5cm (¾in) in diameter

Instructions

Chameleon

Head & body

Round 1: with yarn A and working
into an adjustable ring, 6 dc, join with
sl st (6 sts).

Round 2: 1 ch, 2 dc in each st
around, join with sl st (12 sts).

Round 3: 1 ch, 4 dc, (2 dc in next
st) four times, 4 dc, join with sl st
(16 sts).

Round 4: 1 ch, 7 dc, (2 dc in next st)
twice, 7 dc, join with sl st (18 sts).

Round 5: 1 ch, 6 dc, (2 dc in next st)
six times, 6 dc, join with sl st (24 sts).

Rounds 6–8: 1 ch, 1 dc in each st
around, join with sl st.

Round 9: 1 ch, 9 dc, skip 6 sts, 9 dc,
join with sl st (18 sts).

Round 10: 1 ch, 1 dc in each st
around, join with sl st.

Change to yarn C.

Rounds 11 and 12: 1 ch, 1 dc in
each st around, join with sl st.

Change to yarn B.

Round 13: 1 ch, 7 dc, (2 dc in
next st) four times, 7 dc, join with
sl st (22 sts).

Round 14: 1 ch, 1 dc in each st
around, join with sl st.

Change to yarn A.

Round 15: 1 ch, 1 dc in each st
around, join with sl st.

Round 16: 1 ch, 9 dc, (dc2tog) twice,
9 dc, join with sl st (20 sts).

Change to yarn C.

Round 17: 1 ch, 1 dc in each st
around, join with sl st.

Round 18: 1 ch, 8 dc, (dc2tog) twice,
8 dc, join with sl st (18 sts).

Change to yarn B.

Round 19: 1 ch, 1 dc in each st
around, join with sl st.

Round 20: 1 ch, 7 dc, (dc2tog) twice,
7 dc, join with sl st (16 sts).

Change to yarn A.

Round 21: 1 ch, 6 dc, (dc2tog) twice,
6 dc, join with sl st (14 sts).

Round 22: 1 ch, 5 dc, (dc2tog) twice,
5 dc, join with sl st (12 sts).

Round 23: 1 ch, 4 dc, (dc2tog) twice,
4 dc, join with sl st (10 sts). Stuff.

Round 24: 1 ch, 3 dc, (dc2tog) twice,
3 dc, join with sl st (8 sts).

Rounds 25–27: 1 ch, 1 dc in each st
around, join with sl st.

Round 28: 1 ch, (2 dc, dc2tog) twice,
join with sl st (6 sts).

Fasten off.

Join yarn A to the opening edge of the
head, 1 ch, 6 dc around, join with sl st.

Fasten off.

Leg (make four)

With yarn C, make 6 ch.

Row 1: starting in second ch from
hook, 5 dc, turn (5 sts).

Rows 2–6: 1 ch, 1 dc in each st to
end, turn.

To shape the toes:

Row 7: 1 ch, 2 dc, turn.

Row 8: 1 ch, 2 dc.

Fasten off.

Join yarn to next 2 sts and repeat rows
7 and 8 (leave the last st unworked).

Eye (make two)

Round 1: with yarn D and working
into an adjustable ring, 6 dc, join with
sl st (6 sts).

Fasten off.

Making up

Stitch closed the opening in the head.
Roll the end of the tail and secure the
curl to the body with a few stitches.

Sew an eye piece to each side of the
head. Then, either sew a bead onto the
eye pieces with the black cotton thread,
or embroider French knots onto them
with yarn G.

With yarn E, embroider on the mouth.
Bend each leg, then secure the bent
sections with a few stitches.

Attach the legs to the body.

Weave in any loose ends to finish.

Ladybird

Body

Round 1: with yarn F and working into an adjustable ring, 6 dc, join with sl st (6 sts).

Round 2: 1 ch, 2 dc in each st around, join with sl st (12 sts).

Rounds 3 and 4: 1 ch, dc around, join with sl st. Stuff.

Round 5 (tbl): 1 ch, (dc2tog) six times, join with sl st (6 sts).

Fasten off.

Head

With yarn G and working into an adjustable ring, 4 dc, join with sl st.

Fasten off.

Weave through the finishing tail at the edge to make it into a tiny bobble.

Making up

Weave through the finishing tail at the edge of body. Sew the head to the body. Using yarn G, embroider a line down the middle of the body then make two French knots on each side for the spots.

Puppy

Materials

22m (24yd) of 4-ply (fingering) weight yarn in beige (A)

Small amounts of 4-ply (fingering) weight yarn in soft brown (B), white (C), dark brown (D)

Two 5mm (³⁄₁₆in) black beads, for the eyes

Black cotton thread, for sewing the beads

Toy stuffing

Optional: small amount of black yarn, for embroidering the eyes

Tools

3mm (UK 11, US C2/D3) crochet hook

Chenille needle

All-purpose sewing needle, for sewing on the beads

Scissors

Size

7cm (2¾in)

Instructions

Head

Round 1: with yarn C and working into an adjustable ring, 6 dc, join with a sl st (6 sts).

Round 2: 1 ch, 2 dc in each st around, join with a sl st (12 sts).

Rounds 3 and 4: 1 ch, 1 dc in each st around, join with a sl st.

Change to yarn A.

Round 5: 1 ch, 3 dc, (2 dc in next st) six times, 3 dc, join with a sl st (18 sts).

Round 6: 1 ch, (2 dc, 2 dc in next st) six times, join with a sl st (24 sts).

Rounds 7 and 8: 1 ch, 1 dc in each st around, join with a sl st.

Round 9: 1 ch, (3 dc, 2 dc in next st) six times, join with a sl st (30 sts).

Round 10: 1 ch, 1 dc in each st around, join with a sl st.

Round 11: 1 ch, (3 dc, dc2tog) six times, join with a sl st (24 sts).

Round 12: 1 ch, (2 dc, dc2tog) six times, join with a sl st (18 sts).

Round 13: 1 ch, (1 dc, dc2tog) six times, join with a sl st (12 sts). Stuff.

Round 14: 1 ch, (dc2tog) six times, join with a sl st (6 sts).

Fasten off.

Body

Round 1: with yarn A and working into an adjustable ring, 6 dc, join with a sl st (6 sts).

Round 2: 1 ch, 2 dc in each st around, join with a sl st (12 sts).

Round 3: 1 ch, (1 dc, 2 dc in next st) six times, join with a sl st (18 sts).

Round 4: 1 ch, (2 dc, 2 dc in next st) six times, join with a sl st (24 sts).

Rounds 5–7: 1 ch, 1 dc in each st around, join with a sl st.

Round 8: 1 ch, (2 dc, dc2tog) six times, join with a sl st (18 sts).

Rounds 9–11: 1 ch, 1 dc in each st around, join with a sl st.

Round 12: 1 ch, (1 dc, dc2tog) six times, join with a sl st (12 sts).

Fasten off.

Arm (make two)

Round 1: with yarn A and working into an adjustable ring, 6 dc, join with a sl st (6 sts).

Rounds 2–5: 1 ch, 1 dc in each st around, join with a sl st.

Fasten off leaving a long tail.

Ear (make two)

Round 1: with yarn B and working into an adjustable ring, 5 dc, join with a sl st (5 sts).

Round 2: 1 ch, (2 dc in next st) five times, join with a sl st (10 sts).

Rounds 3 and 4: 1ch, 1dc in each st around, join with a sl st.

Round 5: 1 ch, (3 dc, dc2tog) twice, join with a sl st (8 sts).

Round 6: 1 ch, 1 dc in each st around, join with a sl st.

Round 7: 1 ch, (dc2tog) four times, join with a sl st (4 sts).

Fasten off.

Leg (make two)

Round 1: with yarn A and working into an adjustable ring, 5 dc, join with a sl st (5 sts).

Round 2: 1 ch, 2 dc in each st around, join with a sl st (10 sts).

Round 3: 1 ch, 3 dc, 4 htr, 3 dc, join with a sl st.

Round 4: 1 ch, 3 dc, (htr2tog) twice, 3 dc, join with a sl st (8 sts).

Rounds 5–7: 1 ch, 1 dc in each st around, join with a sl st.

Fasten off.

Tail

With yarn A, 4 ch.

Row 1: starting in second ch from hook, 1 dc in each ch (3 sts).

Round 2: 1 ch, 1 dc in each st.

Fasten off.

Making up

Stuff the body. Attach the head to the body.

Sew eyes onto the head – use the beads and black cotton thread, or make them by embroidering French knots with the black yarn. Embroider the nose using yarn D.

Stuff the arms and legs and attach them. Sew the tail to the body.

Weave in any loose ends to finish.

Turtle

Materials (for one turtle)

Small amounts of 4-ply (fingering) weight yarn in
   light brown (A), pink or green (B), dark pink or blue (C)

Two 4mm (⅛in) black beads, for the eyes

Black cotton thread, for sewing the beads

Toy stuffing

Optional: small amount of black yarn, for embroidering the eyes

Tools

3mm (UK 11, US C2/D3) crochet hook

Chenille needle

All-purpose sewing needle, for sewing on
   the beads

Scissors

Size

9cm (3½in)

Instructions (to make one turtle)

Shell

Round 1: with yarn B and working into an adjustable ring, 6 dc, join with sl st (6 sts).

Round 2: 1 ch, 2 dc in each st around, join with sl st (12 sts).

Keep yarn B on hold. Join yarn C.

Round 3: 1 ch, (1 dc, 2 dc in next st) to end, join with sl st (18 sts).

Round 4: 1 ch, (2 dc in yarn B, 1 dc in yarn B and 1 dc in yarn C both in next st) to end, join with sl st (24 sts).

Round 5: 1 ch, (3 dc in yarn B, 1 dc in yarn B and 1 dc in yarn C both in next st) to end, join with sl st (30 sts).

Keep yarn B on hold. Join in yarn C.

Round 6: with yarn C, 1 ch, (4 dc, 2 dc in next st) to end, join with sl st (36 sts).

Rounds 7–9: 1 ch, (5 dc in yarn B, 1 dc in yarn C) to end, join with sl st.

Cut yarn B. Work with yarn C only.

Round 10: 1 ch, 1 dc in each st around, join with sl st.

Round 11 (tbl): 1 ch, 1 dc in each st around, join with sl st.

Round 12: 1 ch, 1 dc in each st around, join with sl st.

Round 13: 1 ch, (4 dc, dc2tog) to end, join with sl st (30 sts).

Round 14: 1 ch, (3 dc, dc2tog) to end, join with sl st (24 sts).

Round 15: 1 ch, (2 dc, dc2tog) to end, join with sl st (18 sts).

Round 16: 1 ch, (1 dc, dc2tog) to end, join with sl st (12 sts). Stuff.

Round 17: 1 ch, (dc2tog) six times, join with sl st (6 sts).

Fasten off.

Head

Round 1: with yarn A and working into an adjustable ring, 6 dc, join with sl st (6 sts).

Round 2: 1 ch, 2 dc in each st around, join with sl st (12 sts).

Round 3: 1 ch, (1 dc, 2 dc in next st) to end, join with sl st (18 sts).

Rounds 4 and 5: 1 ch, 1 dc in each st around, join with sl st.

Round 6: 1 ch, (1 dc, dc2tog) to end, join with sl st (12 sts).

Round 7: 1 ch, *2 dc, (dc2tog) twice, repeat from * to end, join with sl st (9 sts).

Round 8: 1 ch, 1 dc in each st around, join with sl st.

Fasten off.

Leg (make four)

Round 1: with yarn A and working into an adjustable ring, 5 dc (5 sts).

Round 2: 1 ch, 2 dc in each st around, join with sl st (10 sts).

Round 3: 1 ch, 1 dc in each st around, join.

Round 4: 1 ch, 2 dc, (dc2tog, 2 dc) to end, join with sl st (8 sts). Stuff.

Round 5: 1 ch, (dc2tog) four times, join with sl st (4 sts).

Fasten off.

Tail

With yarn A, make 5 ch.

Row 1: starting in second ch from hook, 4 dc, turn (4 sts).

Row 2: 1 ch, miss first st, 1 dc in each st to end, turn (3 sts).

Row 3: 1 ch, miss first st, 1 dc in each st to end (2 sts).

Fasten off.

Making up

Thread the chenille needle with knotted yarn B. Pierce the centre of the shell from the bottom then take the needle through the shell and out the top. Pull the yarn to flatten base. Bring the needle back through the shell, slightly to the side. Repeat.

Seam the tail with the fastened-off end, then attach the tail to the body.

Stuff the head and attach it to the body. Sew eyes onto the head – use the beads and black cotton thread, or make the eyes by embroidering French knots with the black yarn.

Attach the legs to the body.

Weave through any loose ends to finish.

Owl

Materials (for one owl)

Small amounts of 4-ply (fingering) weight yarn in pink or lilac (A), light brown (B), white (C), yellow (D), dark brown (E)

Toy stuffing

Tools

3mm (UK 11, US C2/D3) crochet hook

Chenille needle

Scissors

Size

6cm (2½in)

Instructions (to make one owl)

Body

Round 1: with yarn A and working into an adjustable ring, 6 dc, join with sl st (6 sts).

Round 2: 1 ch, 2 dc in next st to end, join with sl st (12 sts).

Round 3: 1 ch, (1 dc, 2 dc in next st) to end, join with sl st (18 sts).

Round 4: 1 ch, (2 dc, 2 dc in next st) to end, join with sl st (24 sts).

Round 5: 1 ch, (3 dc, 2 dc in next st) to end, join with sl st (30 sts).

Round 6: 1 ch, (4 dc, 2 dc in next st) to end, join with sl st (36 sts).

Rounds 7 and 8: 1 ch, 1 dc in each st around, join with sl st.

Round 9: 1 ch, (4 dc, dc2tog) to end, join with sl st (30 sts).

Rounds 10–13: 1 ch, 1 dc in each st around, join with sl st.

Round 14: 1 ch, (3 dc, dc2tog) to end, join with sl st (24 sts).

Round 15: 1 ch, 1 dc in each st around, join with sl st.

Round 16: 1 ch, (2 dc, dc2tog) to end, join with sl st (18 sts).

Round 17: 1 ch, 3 dc, (dc2tog, 3 dc) to end, join with sl st (15 sts).

Fasten off.

Wing (make two)

Round 1: with yarn B and working into an adjustable ring, 6 dc, join with sl st (6 sts).

Round 2: 1 ch, 2 dc in each st around, join with sl st (12 sts).

Round 3: 1 ch, 1 dc in each st around, join with sl st.

Round 4: 1 ch, (dc2tog) six times, join with sl st (6 sts).

Round 5: 1 ch, 1 dc in each st around, join with sl st.

Round 6: 1 ch, (dc2tog) three times, join with sl st (3 sts).

Fasten off.

Beak

With yarn D, make 3 ch.

Starting in second ch from hook, 1 sl st, 1 htr.

Fasten off.

Eye (make two)

Round 1: with yarn C and working into an adjustable ring, 6 dc, join with sl st (6 sts).

Round 2: 1 ch, 2 dc in each st around, join with sl st (12 sts).

Fasten off.

Making up

Stuff the body then sew together the fastened-off edge. Attach the wings to the body.

Sew the eye pieces to the head then, with yarn E, embroider the 'V's over each eye. Attach the beak.

To finish, embroider tummy details with yarn B, referring to the photographs.

Weave through any loose ends to finish.

Aeroplane

Materials

Small amounts of 4-ply (fingering)
  weight yarn in yellow (A), green (B),
  coral pink (C), orange (D), white
  (E), sky blue (F), red (G)

Toy stuffing

Tools

3mm (UK 11, US C2/D3)
  crochet hook

Chenille needle

Scissors

Size

10cm (4in) long

Instructions

Plane body

Round 1: with yarn A and working
into an adjustable ring, 6 dc, join with
sl st (6 sts).

Round 2: 1 ch, 2 dc in each st around,
join with sl st (12 sts).

Round 3: 1 ch, (1 dc, 2 dc in next st)
to end, join with sl st (18 sts).

Round 4: 1 ch, 1 dc in each st
around, join with sl st.

Round 5: 1 ch, (2 dc, 2 dc in next st)
to end, join with sl st (24 sts).

Change to yarn B.

Round 6: 1 ch, 1 dc in each st
around, join with sl st.

Round 7: 1 ch, (3 dc, 2 dc in next st)
to end, join with sl st (30 sts).

Rounds 8–11: 1 ch, 1 dc in each st
around, join with sl st.

Round 12: 1 ch, (3 dc, dc2tog) to
end, join with sl st (24 sts).

Rounds 13–16: 1 ch, 1 dc in each st
around, join with sl st.

Round 17: 1 ch, (2 dc, dc2tog) to
end, join with sl st (18 sts).

Rounds 18–22: 1 ch, 1 dc in each st
around, join with sl st.

Round 23: 1 ch, (1 dc, dc2tog) to
end, join with sl st (12 sts).

Round 24: 1 ch, 1 dc in each st
around, join with sl st.

Fasten off.

Wing (make two)

Round 1: with yarn C and working into
an adjustable ring 6 dc, join with sl st
(6 sts).

Round 2: 1 ch, 2 dc in each st around,
join with sl st (12 sts).

Rounds 3 and 4: 1 ch, 1 dc in each
st around, join with sl st.

Round 5: 1 ch, (1 dc, 2 dc in next st)
to end, join with sl st (18 sts).

Rounds 6–9: 1 ch, 1 dc in each st
around, join with sl st.

Fasten off.

Propeller (make three)

Round 1: with yarn E and working
into an adjustable ring, 5 dc, join with
sl st (5 sts).

Round 2: 1 ch, 2 dc in each st
around, join with sl st (10 sts).

Rounds 3 and 4: 1 ch, 1 dc in each
st around, join with sl st.

Round 5: 1 ch, (3 dc, dc2tog) twice,
join with sl st (8 sts).

Round 6: 1 ch, (2 dc, dc2tog) twice,
join with sl st (6 sts).

Round 7: 1 ch, 1 dc in each st
around, join with sl st.

Fasten off.

Front bobble

With yarn G and working into an
adjustable ring, 6 dc, join with sl st
(6 sts).

Round 1: 1 ch, 1 dc in each st around.

Fasten off. Weave through the end to
make the piece into a bobble.

Tail wing (make three)

With yarn D, work as for propeller to
round 2 (10 sts).

Round 3: 1 ch, 1 dc in each st around,
join with sl st.

Round 4: 1 ch, (3 dc, dc2tog) twice,
join with sl st (8 sts).

Fasten off.

Large window (make two)

Round 1: with yarn F and working
into an adjustable ring, 6 dc, join with
sl st (6 sts).

Round 2: 1 ch, 2 dc in each st around,
join with sl st (12 sts).

Fasten off.

Small window (make four)

Work as for large window to round 1.

Fasten off.

Making up

Stuff the plane body then sew together the fastened-off edge. Attach the wings, propellers and tail wings to the plane body.

Attach the front bobble. Attach the windows to the plane body, with the larger windows at the front and the smaller ones towards the back of the plane.

Weave through any loose ends to finish.

Koala

Materials

Small amount of 4-ply (fingering) weight yarn in grey (A)

Tiny amounts of 4-ply (fingering) yarn in aqua blue (B), white (C), yellow (D), dark brown (E)

Two 5mm (³/₁₆in) black beads, for the eyes

Black cotton thread, for sewing the beads

Toy stuffing

Optional: small amount of black yarn, for embroidering the eyes

Tools

3mm (UK 11, US C2/D3) crochet hook

Chenille needle

All-purpose sewing needle, for sewing on the beads

Scissors

Size

9cm (3½in)

Instructions

Note: the body and legs are made in one.

Right leg

Round 1: with yarn A and working into an adjustable ring, 5 dc, join with sl st (5 sts).

Round 2: 1 ch, 2 dc in next st to end, join with sl st (10 sts).

Rounds 3 and 4: 1 ch, 1 dc in each st around, join sl st.

Fasten off.

Left leg

Work as for right leg, do not fasten off. Continue to body.

Body

Round 5: 1 ch, 1 dc in each st around left leg sts, insert hook in first st of right leg and 1 dc in each st around right leg, join with sl st (20 sts).

Round 6: 1 ch, (4 dc, 2 dc in next st) to end, join with sl st (24 sts).

Rounds 7 and 8: 1 ch, 1 dc in each st around, join with sl st.

Round 9: 1 ch, (2 dc, dc2tog) to end, join with sl st (18 sts).

Round 10: 1 ch, 1 dc in each st around, join with sl st.

Round 11: 1 ch, (1 dc, dc2tog) to end, join with sl st (12 sts).

Round 12: 1 ch, 1 dc in each st around, join with sl st.

Fasten off.

Head

Round 1: with yarn A and working into an adjustable ring, 6 dc, join with sl st (6 sts).

Round 2: 1 ch, 2 dc in next st to end, join with sl st (12 sts).

Round 3: 1 ch, (1 dc, 2 dc in next st) to end, join with sl st (18 sts).

Round 4: 1 ch, (2 dc, 2 dc in next st) to end, join with sl st (24 sts).

Round 5: 1 ch, (3 dc, 2 dc in next st) to end, join with sl st (30 sts).

Rounds 6–10: 1 ch, 1 dc in each st around, join with sl st.

Round 11: 1 ch, (3 dc, dc2tog) to end, join with sl st (24 sts).

Rounds 12 and 13: 1 ch, 1 dc in each st around, join with sl st.

Round 14: 1 ch, (2 dc, dc2tog) to end, join with sl st (18 sts).

Round 15: 1 ch, (1 dc, dc2tog) to end, join with sl st (12 sts). Stuff.

Round 16: 1 ch, (dc2tog) six times, join with sl st (6 sts).

Fasten off.

Ear (make two)

Round 1: with yarn A and working into an adjustable ring, 6 dc, join with sl st (6 sts).

Round 2: 1 ch, (2 dc in next st) four times, join yarn C, (2 dc in next st) twice with yarn C, join with sl st (12 sts).

Rounds 3 and 4: keeping colours correct, 1 ch, 1 dc in each st around, join with sl st.

Fasten off.

Arm (make two)

Round 1: with yarn A and working into an adjustable ring, 6 dc, join with sl st (6 sts).

Rounds 2–5: 1 ch, 1 dc in each st around, join with sl st.

Fasten off.

Dungarees – right leg

With yarn B, make 13 ch, join with sl st (12 sts).

Round 1: 1 ch, 1 dc in each st around, join with sl st.

Fasten off.

Dungarees – left leg

Work as for right leg, do not fasten off. Continue to waist.

Dungarees – waist section

Round 2: 1 ch, 1 dc in each st around left leg sts, insert hook in first st of right leg and 1 dc in each st around right leg, join with sl st (24 sts).

Rounds 3 and 4: 1 ch, 1 dc in each st around, join with sl st.

Round 5: 1 ch, (2 dc, dc2tog) to end, join with sl st (18 sts).

Fasten off.

Dungarees–bib

Join yarn to eighth st from last st and 6 dc, turn (6 sts).

Rows 2 and 3: 1 ch, 1 dc in each st.

Fasten off.

Hat

With yarn D, work as for head to round 3 (18 sts).

Round 4: 1 ch, 1 dc in each st around, join with sl st.

Fasten off.

Hat visor

Sl st into sixth st from last st, miss 1 st, 5 dc, sl st in next st.

Fasten off.

Nose

Round 1: with yarn E and working into an adjustable ring, 5 dc, join with sl st (5 sts).

Round 2: 1 ch, 2 dc in next st to end, join with sl st (10 sts).

Round 3: 1 ch, (3 dc, dc2tog) twice, join with sl st (8 sts).

Round 4: 1 ch, (2 dc, dc2tog) twice, join with sl st (6 sts).

Fasten off.

Making up

Stuff the legs and body.

Attach the ears. Sew eyes onto the head – use the beads and black cotton thread, or make the eyes by embroidering French knots with the black yarn.

Attach the nose. With yarn E, embroider a mouth.

Insert stuffing into the hat and then attach it to the head. Attach the head to the body.

Stuff the arms then attach them to body. Pull the dungarees over the body. Make the dungaree straps by threading yarn B through the corners of the bib and crossing the yarn over at the back.

Weave in any loose ends to finish.

Baby Hippo

Materials

30m (33yd) of 4-ply (fingering) weight yarn in pastel pink (A)

Small amount of 4-ply (fingering) weight yarn in light brown (B)

Two 6mm (¼in) black beads, for the eyes

Black cotton thread, for sewing the beads

Toy stuffing

Optional: small amount of black yarn, for embroidering the eyes

Tools

3mm (UK 11, US C2/D3) crochet hook

Chenille needle

All-purpose sewing needle, for sewing on the beads

Scissors

Size

10cm (4in)

Instructions

Body

Round 1: with yarn A and working into an adjustable ring, 6 dc, join with sl st (6 sts).

Round 2: 1 ch, 2 dc in each st around, join with sl st (12 sts).

Round 3: 1 ch, (1 dc, 2 dc in next st) to end, join with sl st (18 sts).

Round 4: 1 ch, (2 dc, 2 dc in next st) to end, join with sl st (24 sts).

Round 5: 1 ch, (3 dc, 2 dc in next st) to end, join with sl st (30 sts).

Rounds 6–10: 1 ch, 1 dc in each st around, join with sl st.

Round 11: 1 ch, (3 dc, dc2tog) to end, join with sl st (24 sts).

Round 12: 1 ch, 1 dc in each st around, join with sl st.

Round 13: 1 ch, (2 dc, dc2tog) to end, join with sl st (18 sts).

Rounds 14–16: 1 ch, 1 dc in each st around, join with sl st.

Round 17: 1 ch, (1 dc, dc2tog) to end, join with sl st (12 sts).

Fasten off.

Head

Work as for body to round 5 (30 sts).

Rounds 6–10: 1 ch, 1 dc in each st around, join with sl st.

Round 11: 1 ch, 6 dc, (1 dc, dc2tog) six times, 6 dc, join with sl st (24 sts).

Round 12: 1 ch, 1 dc in each st around, join with sl st.

Round 13: 1 ch, 6 dc, (dc2tog) six times, 6 dc, join with sl st (18 sts).

Rounds 14–17: 1 ch, 1 dc in each st around, join with sl st.

Round 18: 1 ch, (1 dc, dc2tog) to end, join with sl st (12 sts). Stuff.

Round 19: 1 ch, (dc2tog) six times, join with sl st (6 sts).

Fasten off.

Ear (make two)

Row 1: with yarn A and working into an adjustable ring, 4 htr, turn (4 sts).

Row 2: 1 htr, (2 htr in next st) twice, 1 htr (6 sts).

Fasten off.

Leg (make two)

Round 1: with yarn A and working into an adjustable ring, 6 dc, join with sl st (6 sts).

Round 2: 1 ch, 2 dc in each st around, join with sl st (12 sts).

Rounds 3 and 4: 1 ch, 4 dc, 4 htr, 4 dc, join with sl st.

Round 5: 4 dc, (htr2tog) twice, 4 dc, join with sl st (10 sts).

Rounds 6 and 7: 1 ch, 1 dc in each st around, join with sl st.

Fasten off.

Arm (make two)

Round 1: with yarn A and working into an adjustable ring, 8 dc, join with sl st (8 sts).

Rounds 2–5: 1 ch, 1 dc in each st around, join with sl st.

Fasten off.

Nostril (make two)

With yarn B and working into an adjustable ring, 6 dc, join with sl st.

Fasten off.

Making up

Stuff the body.

Sew the ears to the head. Sew eyes onto the head – use the beads and black cotton thread, or make the eyes by embroidering French knots with the black yarn.

Attach the nostrils to the head. Attach the head to the body.

Stuff the arms and legs and attach them to the body.

Weave in any loose ends to finish.

Nest of Chicks

Materials
(for one chick and the nest)

Small amounts of 4-ply (fingering) weight yarn in pale yellow (A), yellow (B)

Small amount of DK (8-ply/light worsted) weight yarn in variegated brown (C)

Two 3mm (¹⁄₁₆in) black beads, for the eyes

Black cotton thread, for sewing the beads

Toy stuffing

Optional: small amount of black yarn, for embroidering the eyes

Tools

3mm (UK 11, US C2/D3) crochet hook

Chenille needle

All-purpose sewing needle, for sewing on the beads

Scissors

Size

Chicks – 2cm (¾in)

Nest – 6cm (2½in)

Instructions (for one chick and the nest)

Chick

Body

Round 1: with yarn A and working into an adjustable ring, 6 dc, join with sl st (6 sts).

Round 2: 1 ch, 2 dc in each st around, join with sl st (12 sts).

Round 3: 1 ch, (1 dc, 2 dc in next st) to end, join with sl st (18 sts).

Rounds 4–8: 1 ch, 1 dc in each st around, join with sl st.

Round 9: 1 ch, (1 dc, dc2tog) to end, join with sl st (12 sts). Stuff.

Round 10: 1 ch, (dc2tog) six times, join with sl st (6 sts).

Fasten off.

Beak

With yarn B, make 4 ch.

Starting in second ch from hook, sl st, 1 htr, sl st.

Fasten off.

Making up

Attach the beak. Sew eyes onto the head – use the beads and black cotton thread, or make the eyes by embroidering French knots with the black yarn.

Weave in any loose ends to finish.

Nest

Round 1: with yarn C and working into an adjustable ring, 6 dc, join with sl st (6 sts).

Round 2: 1 ch, 2 dc in each st around, join with sl st (12 sts).

Round 3: 1 ch, (1 dc, 2 dc in next st) to end, join with sl st (18 sts).

Round 4: 1 ch, (2 dc, 2 dc in next st) to end, join with sl st (24 sts).

Round 5: 1 ch, (3 dc, 2 dc in next st) to end, join with sl st (30 sts).

Round 6: 1 ch, (4 dc, 2 dc in next st) to end, join with sl st (36 sts).

Round 7: 1 ch, (5 dc, 2 dc in next st) to end, join with sl st (42 sts).

Round 8 (tbl): 1 ch, 1 dc in each st around, join with sl st.

Round 9: 1 ch, 1 dc in each st around, join with sl st.

Fasten off. Weave in any loose ends to finish.

Whales

Materials

Small amounts of 4-ply (fingering) weight yarn in white (A), aqua blue (B), pastel pink (C), grey (D)

Two 6mm (¼in), two 5mm (³⁄₁₆in) and two 4mm (⅛in) black beads, for the eyes

Black cotton thread, for sewing the beads

20cm (8in) length of fine craft wire

Toy stuffing

Optional: small amount of black yarn, for embroidering the eyes

Tools

3mm (UK 11, US C2/D3) crochet hook

Chenille needle

All-purpose sewing needle, for sewing on the beads

Scissors

Pliers

Size (base diameter)

Large – 5cm (2in)

Medium – 4cm (1¾in)

Small – 3.5cm (1½in)

Instructions

Large Blue Whale

Top of the body

Round 1: with yarn B and working into an adjustable ring, 6 dc, join with sl st (6 sts).

Round 2: 1 ch, 2 dc in each st around, join with sl st (12 sts).

Round 3: 1 ch, (1 dc, 2 dc in next st) to end, join with sl st (18 sts).

Round 4: 1 ch, (2 dc, 2 dc in next st) to end, join with sl st (24 sts).

Round 5: 1 ch, (3 dc, 2 dc in next st) to end, join with sl st (30 sts).

Round 6: 1 ch, (4 dc, 2 dc in next st) to end, join with sl st (36 sts).

Rounds 7–13: 1 ch, 1 dc in each st around, join with sl st.

Continue to tail.

Tail

Round 1: 1 ch, 3 dc, make 6 ch, insert hook in the third st away from the first st, 3 dc, join with sl st (12 sts).

Round 2: 1 ch, 1 dc in each st around, join with sl st.

Round 3: 1 ch, (dc2tog) six times, join with sl st (6 sts).

Fasten off.

Base of the body

Round 1: join yarn A to third ch made for the tail, 1 ch, 1 dc in same place

as ch, 1 dc in next 2 ch, 1 dc in each st of body around, 1 dc in next 3 ch, join with sl st (36 sts).

Round 2: 1 ch, (4 dc, dc2tog) to end, join with sl st (30 sts).

Round 3: 1 ch, (3 dc, dc2tog) to end, join with sl st (24 sts).

Round 4: 1 ch, (2 dc, dc2tog) to end, join with sl st (18 sts).

Round 5: 1 ch, (1 dc, dc2tog) to end, join with sl st (12 sts). Stuff.

Round 6: 1 ch, (dc2tog) six times, join with sl st.

Fasten off.

Tail fin (make two)

Round 1: with yarn B and working into an adjustable ring, 8 dc, join with sl st (8 sts).

Round 2: 1 ch, 2 tr in each st around, join with sl st (16 sts).

Fasten off.

Making up

Sew the tail fins to the end of the tail.

Sew eyes onto the head – use the two 6mm (¼in) beads and black cotton thread, or make them by embroidering French knots with the black yarn.

To make the jet of water at the top of the head, cut the length of wire to measure 7cm (3in) and wrap it with yarn A. Bend the length in half, then insert the folded end into the top of

the head. Secure the wire with yarn A, threading it around the wire and through the body.

Medium Pink Whale

Top of the body

Using yarn C, work as for the Large Blue Whale to round 5 (30 sts).

Rounds 6–11: 1 ch, 1 dc in each st around, join with sl st.

Continue to tail.

Tail

Round 1: 1 ch, 2 dc, make 4 ch, insert hook in two sts away from the first st, 2 dc, join with sl st (8 sts).

Round 2: 1 ch, 1 dc in each st around, join with sl st.

Fasten off.

Base of the body

Round 1: join yarn A to second ch of tail, 1 ch, 1 dc in same place as ch, 1 dc in next ch, 1 dc in each st to end, 1 dc in next 2 ch, join with sl st (30 sts).

Work as rounds 3–6 of the base of the Large Blue Whale.

Fasten off.

Tail fin (make two)

Round 1: with yarn C and working into an adjustable ring, 8 dc, join with sl st (8 sts).

Round 2: 1 ch, 2 dc in each st around, join with sl st (16 sts).

Fasten off.

Making up

Make up in the same way as the Large Blue Whale, using the two 5mm (³⁄₁₆in) beads and a 6cm (2¼in) length of wire.

Small Grey Whale

Top of the body

With yarn D, work as for Large Blue Whale to Round 4 (24 sts). Stuff.

Rounds 5–9: 1 ch, 1 dc in each st around, join with sl st.

Continue to tail.

Tail

Round 1: 1 ch, 2 dc, make 3 ch, insert hook in two sts away from the first st, 2 dc, join with sl st (7 sts).

Fasten off.

Base

Round 1: join yarn A to second ch of the tail, 1 ch, 1 dc in same place as ch, 1 dc in next ch, 1 dc in each st of body, 1 dc in last ch, join with sl st (24 sts).

Work as Rounds 4–6 of the base of the Large Blue Whale.

Tail fin (make two)

With yarn D and working into an adjustable ring, 3 ch, 8 tr, sl st in third ch to join.

Fasten off.

Making up

Make up in the same way as the Large Blue Whale, using the two 4mm (⅛in) beads and a 5cm (2in) length of wire.

Rabbit

Materials

Small amounts of 4-ply (fingering) weight yarn in white (A)

Tiny amounts of 4-ply (fingering) weight yarn in pink (B), yellow (C), soft brown (D)

Two 4mm (⅛in) black beads, for the eyes

Black cotton thread, for sewing the beads

Toy stuffing

Optional: small amount of black yarn, for embroidering the eyes

Tools

3mm (UK 11, US C2/D3) crochet hook

Chenille needle

All-purpose sewing needle, for sewing on the beads

Scissors

Size

9cm (3½in)

Instructions

Note: the body and legs are made in one.

Right leg

Round 1: with yarn A and working into an adjustable ring, 5 dc, join with sl st (5 sts).

Round 2: 1 ch, 2 dc in each st around, join with sl st (10 sts).

Rounds 3–4: 1 ch, 1 dc in each st around, join with sl st.

Fasten off.

Left leg

Work as for right leg, but do not fasten off after round 4. Continue to body.

Body

Round 5: 1 ch, 1 dc in each st around left leg sts, insert hook in first st of right leg and 1 dc in each st around right leg, join with sl st (20 sts).

Round 6: 1 ch, (4 dc, 2 dc in next st) to end, join with sl st (24 sts).

Rounds 7–8: 1 ch, 1 dc in each st around, join with sl st.

Round 9: 1 ch, (2 dc, dc2tog) to end, join with sl st (18 sts).

Round 10: 1 ch, 1 dc in each st around, join with sl st.

Round 11: 1 ch, (1 dc, dc2tog) to end, join with sl st (12 sts).

Round 12: 1 ch, 1 dc in each st around, join.

Fasten off.

Head

Round 1: with yarn A and working into an adjustable ring, 6 dc, join with sl st (6 sts).

Round 2: 1 ch, 2 dc in each st around, join with sl st (12 sts).

Round 3: 1 ch, (1 dc, 2 dc in next st) to end, join with sl st (18 sts).

Round 4: 1 ch, (2 dc, 2 dc in next st) to end, join with sl st (24 sts).

Round 5: 1 ch, (3 dc, 2 dc in next st) to end, join with sl st (30 sts).

Rounds 6–10: 1 ch, 1 dc in each st around, join with sl st.

Round 11: 1 ch, (3 dc, dc2tog) to end, join with sl st (24 sts).

Rounds 12 and 13: 1 ch, 1 dc in each st around, join with sl st.

Round 14: 1ch, (2 dc, dc2tog) to end, join with sl st (18 sts).

Round 15: 1 ch, (1 dc, dc2tog) to end, join with sl st (12 sts). Stuff.

Round 16: 1 ch, (dc2tog) six times, join with sl st (6 sts).

Fasten off.

Ear (make two)

Round 1: with yarn A and working into an adjustable ring, 5 dc, join with sl st (5 sts).

Round 2: 1 ch, (2 dc in next st) three times, join yarn B, (2 dc in next st) twice with yarn B, join with sl st (10 sts).

Rounds 3–7: keeping colours as set, 1 ch, 1 dc into each st around, join with sl st.

Fasten off.

Arm (make two)

Round 1: with yarn A and working into an adjustable ring, 6 dc, join with sl st (6 sts).

Rounds 2–5: 1 ch, 1 dc in each st around, join with sl st.

Fasten off.

Dress

With yarn B, make 13 ch, sl st in first ch to join (12 sts).

Round 1: 1 ch, (1 dc, 2 dc in next st) to end, join with sl st (18 sts).

Round 2: join yarn C, with yarn C, 1 ch, 1 dc in each st around, join with sl st.

Round 3: with yarn B, (2 dc, 2 dc in next st) to end, join with sl st (24 sts).

Round 4: with yarn C, 1 ch, 1 dc in each st around, join with sl st.

Round 5: with yarn B, 1 ch, 1 dc in each st around, join with sl st.

Round 6: with yarn C, 1 ch, 2 htr in each st around, join with sl st (48 sts).

Fasten off.

Making up

Attach the ears to the head. Sew eyes onto the head – use the beads and black cotton thread, or make the eyes by embroidering French knots with the black yarn. With yarn D, embroider a French knot for the nose.

Stuff the body and pull the dress over the body.

Attach the head to the body. Stuff the arms then attach them to body.

Weave in any loose ends to finish.

Cupcake

Materials

Small amounts of 4-ply (fingering) weight yarn in pink or mint green (A), white (B), light brown (C)

Small amount of DK (8-ply/light worsted) weight yarn in dark pink (D)

Toy stuffing

Tools

3mm (UK 11, US C2/D3) crochet hook

Chenille needle

All-purpose sewing needle, for sewing on the beads

Scissors

Size

6cm (2½in)

Instructions

Cake

Round 1: with yarn C and working into an adjustable ring, 6 dc, join with sl st (6 sts).

Round 2: 1 ch, 2 dc in each st around, join with sl st (12 sts).

Round 3: 1 ch, (1 dc, 2 dc in next st) to end, join with sl st (18 sts).

Round 4: 1 ch, (2 dc, 2 dc in next st) to end, join with sl st (24 sts).

Round 5: 1 ch, (3 dc, 2 dc in next st) to end, join with sl st (30 sts).

Round 6 (tbl): 1 ch, 1 dc in each st around, join with sl st.

Rounds 7–12: 1 ch, 1 dc in each st around, join with sl st.

Fasten off.

Cream

With yarn A, make 21 ch.

Row 1: starting in second ch from hook, 1 dc in each st to end (20 sts).

Row 2 (tbl): 1 ch, 2 dc in first st, 1 dc in each st to last 2 sts, dc2tog.

Join yarn B.

Row 3 (tbl): With yarn B, 1 ch, dc2tog, 1 dc in each st to last st, 2 dc in last st.

Row 4: work as row 2.

Work two rows in yarn A, two rows in yarn B, increasing 1 st on one end, decreasing 1 st on the other. Repeat until you have six blocks in each yarn colour.

Fasten off.

Cherry

Round 1: with yarn D and working into an adjustable ring, 6 dc, join with sl st (6 sts).

Round 2: 1 ch, 2 dc in each st around, join with sl st (12 sts).

Round 3: 1 ch, 1 dc in each st around, join with sl st. Stuff.

Round 4: 1 ch, (dc2tog) six times, join with sl st (6 sts).

Fasten off.

Stem

With yarn D, make 4 ch. Starting in second ch from hook, sl st in each st (3 sts).

Fasten off.

Making up

Sew the cream together along the first and last row edges, placing different colours together alternately to create a stripy effect.

Once you have created a ring with the cream pieces, weave a length of yarn through one of the side edges then pull gently to gather the edge. Insert toy stuffing into the top, ungathered side. Work another length of yarn along the other side edge and pull tightly to close the 'top' of the cream piece.

Insert toy stuffing into the cake. Place the stuffed cream piece on top then secure the cream to the cake with yarn B, sewing small stitches all around the top edge of the cake.

Sew the cherry on top of the cream. Sew the stem onto the cherry.

Weave in any loose ends to finish.

Squirrel

Materials

30m (33yd) of DK (8-ply/light worsted) weight yarn in red brown (A)

Small amounts of DK (8-ply/light worsted) weight yarn in white (B), dark brown (C)

Two 6mm (¼in) black beads, for the eyes

Black cotton thread, for sewing the beads

Toy stuffing

Optional: small amount of black yarn, for embroidering the eyes

Tools

3mm (UK 11, US C2/D3) crochet hook

Chenille needle

All-purpose sewing needle, for sewing on the beads

Scissors

4cm (1½in) pompom maker

Size

9cm (3½in)

Instructions

Head

Round 1: with yarn A and working into an adjustable ring, 6 dc, join with sl st (6 sts).

Round 2: 1 ch, 1 dc in each st around, join with sl st.

Round 3: 1 ch, 2 dc in each st around, join with sl st (12 sts).

Round 4: 1 ch, 1 dc in each st around, join with sl st.

Round 5: 1 ch, (1 dc, 2 dc in next st) to end, join with sl st (18 sts).

Round 6: 1 ch, 1 dc in each st around, join with sl st.

Round 7: 1 ch, (2 dc, 2 dc in next st) to end, join with sl st (24 sts).

Rounds 8–10: 1 ch, 1 dc in each around, join with sl st.

Round 11: 1 ch, (2 dc, dc2tog) to end, join with sl st (18 sts).

Round 12: 1 ch, (1 dc, dc2tog) to end, join with sl st (12 sts). Stuff.

Round 13: 1 ch, (dc2tog) six times, join with sl st (6 sts).

Fasten off.

Ear (make two)

With yarn A, make 5 ch.

Row 1: starting in second ch from hook, 1 dc in each ch, turn (4 sts).

Row 2: 1 ch, 1 dc in each st to end, turn.

Row 3: 1 ch, (htr2tog) twice (2 sts). Fasten off.

Body

Round 1: with yarn B and working into an adjustable ring, 6 dc, join with sl st (6 sts).

Round 2: 1 ch, 2 dc in each st around, join with sl st (12 sts).

Round 3: 1 ch, (1 dc, 2 dc in next st) to end, join with sl st (18 sts).

Change to yarn A.

Round 4: 1 ch, (2 dc, 2 dc in next st) to end, join with sl st (24 sts).

Rounds 5–9: 1 ch, 1 dc in each st around, join with sl st.

Round 10: 1 ch, (2 dc, dc2tog) to end, join with sl st (18 sts).

Round 11: 1 ch, (1 dc, dc2tog) to end, join with sl st (12 sts). Stuff.

Round 12: 1 ch, (dc2tog) six times, join with sl st (6 sts).

Fasten off.

Leg (make two)

With yarn A, make 11 ch.

Row 1: starting in second ch from hook, 1 dc in each ch, turn (10 sts).

Rows 2 and 3: 1 ch, 1 dc in each dc to end, turn.

Row 4: 1 ch, (3 dc, dc2tog) to end, turn (8 sts).

Row 5: 1 ch, (2 dc, dc2tog) to end, turn (6 sts).

Row 6: 1 ch, 1 dc in each st to end. Fasten off.

Arm (make two)

With yarn A, make 9 ch.

Row 1: starting in second ch from hook, 1 dc in each ch, turn (8 sts).

Rows 2 and 3: 1 ch, 1 dc in each dc to end, turn.

Row 4: 1 ch, (2 dc, dc2tog) to end, turn (6 sts).

Row 5: 1 ch, 1 dc in each st to end.

Fasten off.

Tail

Using the 4cm (1½in) pompom maker and yarn A, wind the yarn approximately 80–90 times around each side. Tie the two sides together and release the pompom, then trim the pompom into an oval shape. Leave the length of yarn tied around the middle of the pompom untrimmed, to use for sewing later.

Making up

Attach the ears to the head. Sew eyes onto the head – use the beads and black cotton thread, or make the eyes by embroidering French knots with the black yarn. Embroider the nose onto the head with yarn C. Attach the head to the body.

Fold an arm in half lengthways, right sides facing, and sew the long edges together. Turn the arm right side out then stuff. Repeat with the other arm, and for both legs. Attach the arms and legs to the body. Attach the pompom tail.

Weave in any loose ends to finish.

Acknowledgements
I would like to thank everyone on the Search Press team,
especially Katie French and Emily Adam, for helping me to
create such a wonderful book. I would also like to thank the
designer, Emma Sutcliffe, for the beautiful layout and the
photographer, Fiona Murray, for the lovely photography.
A big thanks also to Clover Mfg. Co. Ltd for kindly supplying
the tools.